FAITH IN THE FAMILY

SHARING OUR FAITH WITH OUR CHILDREN

David Durston

with

Chris Hughes, Dave Bingham and David Osborne

Series editor: Tim Carr

BRITISH AND FOREIGN BIBLE SOCIETY
Stonehill Green, Westlea, Swindon SN5 7DG, England

First published 1991

British Library Cataloguing in Publication Data
Faith in the family
1. Faith
I. Durston, David
249

ISBN 0-564-05745-2

Printed in Great Britain by Stanley L. Hunt (Printers) Ltd.

Bible Societies exist to provide resources for Bible distribution and use. Bible Society in England and Wales (BFBS) is a member of the United Bible Societies, an international partnership working in over 180 countries.

Their common aim is to reach all people with the Bible, or some part of it, in a language they can understand and at a price they can afford. Parts of the Bible have now been translated into approximately 1,900 languages. Bible Societies aim to help every church at every point where it uses the Bible. You are invited to share in this work by your prayers and gifts. The Bible Society in your country will be very happy to provide details of its activity.

CONTENTS

Anyone is free to look at the notes for leaders of
Faith in the Family
groups on pages 45–55.
Leaders should study them carefully.

WELCOME

Welcome to this *Faith in the Family* group. You have responsibility for a child or some children. You are a parent, or perhaps you are a Sunday School teacher, an uncle, an aunt or a grandparent, or you look after children in other ways. You would like to share with these children your faith in God and in Jesus Christ. Like many other people, you probably do not find this easy, but you believe it is very important. In the group you will be meeting with other people who are wrestling with the same difficulties.

God has made us all individuals. Every person is unique. In every family, in every situation, we have to work out how to share our faith. The group will provide a chance to work things out together, to help one another at difficult points, to encourage one another when it is hard going. There are no easy answers. If there were, someone would have found them a long time ago.

A DIFFERENT KIND OF LEARNING

People who join a group hoping to learn something often come expecting to be taught. They come looking to the leaders to give them answers. This group has a different approach. It gives you a chance to explore your own experience together, with the Bible to guide and help you. Your experience is very important. You can learn a great deal from it. When you share it with others, they can learn from it too, just as you can learn from theirs. The rule is: the more you share together, the more you all gain.

Your feelings play an important part in helping you to learn, or stopping you from learning. Feelings matter, so don't hide them, even if sometimes it is uncomfortable expressing them.

Our feelings can help us to understand the Bible better. They help us to enter more deeply into the meaning of what it contains. The Bible helps us to put our thoughts and feelings in a wider context. We see connections with what people in the Bible thought and felt and said.

If other people in the group are to be free to say what they really thought and felt and did, they will need to feel safe in doing so. They will want to know you will accept them and not be critical of them. Your reactions will matter as well as the leaders'.

You may well find it helpful to bring a notebook and pencil to meetings so that you can write down your thoughts and remember them afterwards.

A PROVERB FROM THE BIBLE

Beg for knowledge; plead for insight. Look for it as hard as you would for silver or some hidden treasure. If you do, you will know what it means to fear the LORD and you will succeed in learning about God.

Proverbs 2.3–5

That makes learning sound rather like hard work. You have to put your heart into it. But looking for treasure can be very exciting. We hope you will find this group exciting too.

FIRST MEETING

INTRODUCTIONS

AIM

To help everyone to feel "at home" in the group, and to look forward to the group meetings.

Welcome to the group meeting. It may be that most of the other people in the group are strangers to you, that you are in a place where you have never been before and that you are not sure what you have let yourself in for. If you are feeling awkward and nervous, probably some of the others are as well. We hope that at the end of this session you will feel "at home" with them, that they will feel "at home" in the group too, and that you will all be looking forward to the rest of the meetings.

In this meeting you will be invited to explore and share something of who you are. Do not feel you have to say more than you want to. If you feel others are a little shy, gently encourage them by asking them one or two questions about themselves or their children.

As well as introducing you to the main subject of the course, this first meeting will help you to get the "feel" of it. An essential part of it is that your experience is important. You will be learning by thinking back over what is happening to you, and from the experience of others in the group, and you will be helping them to learn. In the group discussions the Bible will serve as a guide for you all.

A NOTE ABOUT PRAYER

Prayer in the family is the subject of the fifth meeting. The group, however, needs to spend some time in this meeting discussing what place (if any) prayer will have in its life, and perhaps working out a form which has general agreement and does not leave anyone feeling uncomfortable. This may mean, for example, that some members accept a form of prayer that is shorter and more formal than they would have chosen. Don't underestimate the importance of this discussion of prayer and working towards an agreement in setting the tone for the life of the group.

REMEMBER

Within the group, share something of who you are, and who your children are. It may help to break the ice if the leaders speak first. It is probably best not to go round in order, but to allow members of the group to open up at their own speed.

(Time guide 15 minutes)

The leaders will introduce the course, the subjects of the sessions and the approach. If there is anything that you find difficult to understand, or anything that is not mentioned but you would like to know about, please ask. If there are some things you are particularly looking forward to, or hope to get out of these meetings, share your hopes with the rest of the group.

(Time guide 10 minutes)

Individually, think of one or two religious experiences you had as a child, and then, in pairs, share them with a partner and listen to their experiences. Allow yourself and your partner five minutes each. The leaders will help you to keep time.

(Time guide 10 minutes)

Questions that may help you to describe these experiences include:

How old were you? Where were you? What happened? What did you feel? Why do you think it made an impression on you?

REFLECT

Come together as a group and discuss:
From the experience you described, what is it like being a child?

(Time guide 15 minutes)

It may help if this question is written on a large sheet of paper and put up where everyone can see it.

Call out the words or phrases that occur to you. One of the leaders will write them on a sheet, and then put them up where you can all see them. You can then go through them and invite people to say why they suggested them. Others may want to qualify them, e.g. "That's true for some children, but it wouldn't have applied to me."

COMPARE

Individually, look at these short passages from the Bible. Do any of them remind you of what you were like as a child?

(Time guide 5 minutes)

Children are a gift from the LORD; they are a real blessing.
Psalm 127.3

If a child has his own way, he will make his mother ashamed of him.
Proverbs 29.15

There was once a man who had two sons. He went to the elder one and said, "Son, go and work in the vineyard today."

5

"I don't want to," he answered, but later he changed his mind and went. Then the father went to the other son and said the same thing. "Yes, sir," he answered, but he did not go. Which one of the two did what his father wanted?

Matthew 21.28–30

Is there anything you would like to share with other members of the group? There is no need for you to say anything, but if you want to tell the others something about your childhood, you can. Someone else may want to share something with you.

(Time guide 5 minutes)

REFLECT AGAIN

Think of one occasion which has helped you to learn and grow as a person, an experience which has given you a new awareness of the meaning and purpose of your life, or a new understanding of your relationship with God. It may not have been anything to do with religion. For example an illness, or the death of a friend, may have caused you to change your attitude to life or to ambition. It may have been either as a child or as an adult.

In pairs, describe your experience to each other—five minutes each. *(Time guide 10 minutes)*

Then come together as a group and discuss:

From the experience you have described, what were the things that helped you to learn? What hindered you? How far are these similar for adults and children? Or different?

(Time guide 15 minutes)

Discuss what place you want prayer to have in the group. The paragraph in the introduction to this meeting may help here.

(Time guide 10 minutes)

End the meeting with prayer, if appropriate.

BEFORE THE NEXT MEETING

Try to recall two incidents that are somehow typical of how your child gets on with you.

One of these will be about *the good, positive side* of the way your child gets on with you. The other will be about *the awkward or difficult side* of your relationship.

If you have more than one child, think of two incidents for each child. (If you have several children there will probably not be time for you to tell all your incidents, so you will need to decide which you are going to tell first.) You may like to jot something down in your notebook to help you remember.

If you can bring an object, like a favourite toy, a drawing, or a book, and explain what it means to your child and to you, that would be very interesting.

GROUP GUIDELINES

Think about these guidelines for being a member of a *Faith in the Family* group. If you like you can tick those things you are prepared to do to the best of your ability.

1. Everyone has something to contribute, so:
   - [ ] we are going to encourage each other to speak;
   - [ ] we are going to listen sensitively to each other;
   - [ ] we are going to take the risk of making our own contribution.

2. Everyone has something to learn, including the leaders, so:
   - [ ] we are going to help each other to appreciate new ways of looking at things, and try out new ways of responding to situations.

3. ☐ This course is based on the principle of learning by reflecting on experience, so:

   ☐ we expect to learn by working out new understanding for ourselves;

   ☐ we do not expect to be given answers;

   ☐ we may decide to change the way we have always believed or acted.

4. Disagreement is acceptable and may be helpful in working out new understanding, so:

   ☐ we are going to say so if we honestly disagree with others;

   ☐ we are not going to resent it if others disagree with us;

   ☐ we are always going to try to understand why we disagree.

5. The expression of feeling is acceptable, including negative feelings which may seem to be destructive, so:

   ☐ we are going to be as open as we can in saying what we feel, and respect others for their honesty.

Second Meeting

Our Children

Aim

To identify the different types of exchanges and relationships adults have with their children, both positive and negative.

Introduction

Working in pairs may help open discussion of this subject in an unthreatening situation, and may also allow members to discover that they face similar difficulties.

Remember

In pairs, share the incidents with your children that you have chosen, both those about the good, positive side and those about the awkward or negative side. Allow each partner fifteen minutes. (Half an hour is a long time to talk in pairs, and it will be helpful if the leaders can let members know when, say, ten, fifteen, and twenty-five minutes have passed.)

(Time guide 30 minutes)

Reflect

As a group, give single words or short phrases that sum up the positive and negative sides of your relationships with your children, and write these on a chart or wallsheet. When everyone who is willing to speak has contributed, put up the sheet where everyone can see it, and comment on such points as:

- anything that surprised you;
- anything you found it helpful to say or hear;
- anything that came up again and again.

(Time guide 10 minutes)

COMPARE

This part of the session compares our role as parents with God's role as the father of his people. The passage from Hosea should provide some interesting comparisons.

Read the introduction and the Bible passage silently, and then let one member read it aloud to the whole group. Think about the questions silently for a few minutes before beginning to share your answers.

(Time guide 20 minutes)

T he people of Israel looked back to the escape from Egypt (the Exodus) as the great event in their national history. They had been slaves in Egypt, building palaces and pyramids for harsh slave-drivers, but by God's grace they were liberated. Through that escape and the long journey across the Sinai desert they were welded together as a nation.

At the time when Hosea was writing, Israel was a small and weak nation, threatened by more powerful nations to the north and south. They had experienced an enemy army invading, smashing down and burning their places of worship and killing their priests. They knew there was a real possibility of it happening again. Hosea sees this as God's judgement on the people for turning their backs on him.

10

The LORD says,
"When Israel was a child, I loved him
and called him out of Egypt as my son.
But the more I called to him,
the more he turned away from me.
My people sacrificed to Baal;
they burnt incense to idols.
Yet I was the one who taught Israel to walk.
I took my people up in my arms,
but they did not acknowledge that I took care of them.
I drew them to me with affection and love.
I picked them up and held them to my cheek;
I bent down to them and fed them.

They refuse to return to me, and so they must return to Egypt,
and Assyria will rule them. War will sweep through their cities
and break down the city gates. It will destroy my people because
they do what they themselves think best. They insist on turning
away from me. They will cry out because of the yoke that is on
them, but no one will lift it from them.

"How can I give you up, Israel?
How can I abandon you?
Could I ever destroy you as I did Admah,
or treat you as I did Zeboiim?
My heart will not let me do it!
My love for you is too strong.
I will not punish you in my anger;
I will not destroy Israel again.
For I am God and not man.
I, the Holy One, am with you.
I will not come to you in anger."

Hosea 11.1–9

QUESTIONS FOR DISCUSSION

- What are the actions and words by which the people of Israel show their attitude to God?

11

- What are the actions and words by which God shows his attitude to his people?

When you have worked out your answers to these questions, then ask yourselves:
- In what way do our children treat us as the people of Israel treated the Lord?
- In what way do we feel towards them as God does towards his people?

RESPOND

The leader should put up these questions on a sheet where everyone can see them:
- is there one thing you want to remember from this evening?
- is there one thing you want to do as a result of it?

Think about the questions in silence and then share in pairs any thoughts you have.

(Time guide 15 minutes)

Anybody who has something to say to the group can do so now, but if nobody wants to, it does not matter.

(Time guide 5 minutes)

Close the meeting with prayer, if appropriate.

BEFORE THE NEXT MEETING

At the end of each of the following meetings we are going to suggest a number of things you can do with your children to get ready for the next meeting. If you have not already told your children that you are coming to the group and what it is about, it might be helpful to tell them this week. Let them know why you joined the group. Ask them if they would be willing to help you to get ready for the next meeting. Call it your "homework" if you like. That might get you some sympathy!

Work out what kind of involvement your children have with the Bible in a typical week. Talk with them about whether it is used in school. Think about how it is used at home and in the church. Be aware of different ways in which your children come into contact with it. For example, do you have posters or calendars with Bible quotations at home or at church?

If you can, try to get them to talk about how they feel about the Bible. You might ask: what do you find interesting in it? When do you like to read it? Do you prefer having it read to you? What is your favourite story? What do you not like about the Bible?

If they show any interest, it will be important that you share with them how you use the Bible and what interests you in it.

As you talk with them, remember that children's feelings about the Bible may be an expression of their feelings about the adults who bring them in contact with the Bible. If they do not like their teacher they may say they dislike everything he or she values. If they are cross with you for stopping them from watching television, they may say the Bible is boring as a way of getting back at you.

Finally, please collect together the Bible booklets or story books that your children enjoy, or used to enjoy when they were younger, and bring them with you to the meeting. Other members may be delighted to see what you have, and you may be just as interested in what they bring.

Third Meeting

Sharing the Bible with our Children

Aim

To help you to be aware of the variety of ways in which the Bible can be used with children, so that they are helped to use it and enjoy it for themselves.

Introduction

The Bible is our central resource for knowing God's love and his plan for us, and for increasing our understanding of the Christian life. During this session the group will be examining various ways of using the Bible, particularly with children, and exploring which of these has value. It may be that some uses of the Bible are rejected by the group as a whole. Such uses should be dropped from the list. If a way of using the Bible is rejected by some but not all of the group members it should be retained, with an acknowledgement of the diversity of opinion in the group.

Remember

As a group, remember how you have used the Bible (in church, at home, in groups). Some suggestions are given later in the session (see pages 18–19).

Make a list of these on a flipchart or wallsheet.

(Time guide 10 minutes)

REFLECT

As a group, consider the advantages and disadvantages of each.

(Time guide 20 minutes)

COMPARE

In pairs, look at the Bible passages that follow.

(Time guide 10 minutes)

T he Bible is a library of 66 books. Some were written by one author; others are collections of pieces written over hundreds of years. If the Bible were separated into its different books they might be placed in different parts of your local library — for example history, poetry, law, letters. Which part of the library would you place each of these in? You may wish to underline words and phrases that help you to understand the different reasons why these books were written.

All the people of Israel were listed according to their families, and this information was recorded in The Book of the Kings of Israel.

1 Chronicles 9.1

Everything else that King Josiah did is recorded in The History of the Kings of Judah.

2 Kings 23.28

This book contains the messages about Judah and Jerusalem which God revealed to Isaiah son of Amoz during the time when Uzziah, Jotham, Ahaz, and Hezekiah were Kings of Judah.

Isaiah 1.1

16

Come, let us praise the LORD!
Let us sing for joy to God, who protects us!
Let us come before him with thanksgiving
* and sing joyful songs of praise.*
Psalm 95.1,2

The proverbs of Solomon son of David and king of Israel.
Here are proverbs that will help you to recognize wisdom and
good advice, and understand sayings with deep meaning.
Proverbs 1.1,2

Dear Theophilus:
Many people have done their best to write a report of the things
that have taken place among us. They wrote what we have been
told by those who saw these things from the beginning and who
proclaimed the message. And so, your Excellency, because
I have carefully studied all these matters from their beginning,
I thought it would be good to write an orderly account for you.
I do this so that you will know the full truth about everything
which you have been taught.
Luke 1.1–4

From Paul . . . to the churches of Galatia: may God our Father
and the Lord Jesus Christ give you grace and peace . . . See
what big letters I make as I write to you now with my own hand!
. . . May the grace of our Lord Jesus Christ be with you all, my
brothers. Amen.
Galatians 1.1–3, 6.11,18

In the past, God spoke to our ancestors many times and in
many ways through the prophets, but in these last days he has
spoken to us through his son.
Hebrews 1.1,2

. . . ever since you were a child, you have known the Holy
Scriptures, which are able to give you the wisdom that leads to
salvation through faith in Christ Jesus. All Scripture is inspired
by God and is useful for teaching the truth, rebuking error,
correcting faults, and giving instruction for right living . . .
2 Timothy 3.15,16

Come together as a group again, go back to the list on the wallsheet, and consider which ways of using the Bible would be suitable for:

- a child on his or her own;
- an adult and a child together;
- a family;
- a group of children, e.g. a Sunday School class in church.

Can you find any new ideas about how you can use the Bible with your children? Can you offer any suggestions to other people in the group?

(Time guide 30 minutes)

RESPOND

In pairs, talk about these possibilities, and tell each other of any ways of using the Bible with your children that you hope to try out. Write down any ideas that you want to remind yourself of.

(Time guide 10 minutes)

Close the meeting with prayer, if appropriate.

SOME WAYS OF USING THE BIBLE

Prayer   The Lord's Prayer, the Grace, Psalms, Mary's Song of Praise, and many other prayers are contained in the Bible.

Storytelling   A retelling of the Bible story can be read (e.g. Kossoff, Dickinson, Knowles etc — see list of resources, pages 57–59), or the story can be freshly told. The latter is generally the most effective with children.

Play   Particularly effective with the Gospels, but also other narratives. Keep to a simple plot, and replay several times, giving different children a chance to be Jesus, the blind beggar, the centurion etc. If possible discuss after the game. Ask: how do you think the blind man felt? Did you enjoy being led? etc.

Dramatic production This is different from playing. Here a script is used, and rehearsed. It is important to help children to get into parts. Again, discussion afterwards is valuable.

Memory Bible passages can be learnt by heart.

Liturgy The Bible is read in nearly all church services.

Singing Many psalms and other parts of the Bible were composed to be sung, and are often sung in church services.

Historical study Passages and books can be studied historically. When were they written? What was happening at that time? How did they come into their present form? What was society like at the time? etc.

Literary study Books and passages can also be studied from a literary angle, seeing the type of literature they are; how the writer conveys his message; his sources and his literary background.

Schemes There are various schemes to assist with daily Bible reading. These are available for different age groups and abilities, from organizations such as Scripture Union and the Bible Reading Fellowship.

Quizzes Bible quizzes are popular with some children, particularly those with good mental recall.

Themes Different passages can be grouped under themes, e.g. people who were helped by Jesus; calls for repentance; comforting texts in times of anxiety etc.

Proof texts Some people find it helpful to group together isolated sentences ("texts") to produce an argument or to evoke a particular type of feeling.

BEFORE THE NEXT MEETING

In the next meeting we will be looking at the way in which conflicts and anger develop in family life, and thinking about the kind of things we might do to sort them out.

Over the coming week try to keep a record of the conflicts which develop between yourself and your children and the ways in which they were resolved. You may like to write it in your notebook to help you remember.

Also have a chat with your children. Ask them about the things that happen at home which cause them to feel angry. If your children are too young for this type of discussion make a note of the situations in which they lose their temper, and what it was that triggered their anger.

FOURTH MEETING

CONFLICT AND ANGER IN THE FAMILY

AIM

To enable you to learn from your own experience in the family, both as a child and as a parent.

INTRODUCTION

Conflicts between parents and children are a normal part of family life. They are often disturbing and sometimes painful. They can be destructive of family life. On the other hand, through conflicts children and young people learn about living in relationship with others, and develop attitudes and values which they make their own. Through clashes with their parents, adolescents develop a sense of their own autonomy and identity.

The activities have been designed to enable you

- to put your feelings into words in such a way as to understand more clearly why you feel (or felt) as you do (did);
- to reflect on how conflicts have been resolved or aggravated, so as to understand the factors that tend to resolve conflicts, or cause them to fester or be aggravated.

It is often difficult to reflect on strong feelings. One may only be able to describe them with a simple word, such as "upset", "furious". Reflection may uncover an underlying feeling that has given rise to the anger or upset. At times the way someone tells their story may give clues to this underlying feeling.

The session does not suggest any rules that can be laid down in order to avoid or resolve conflicts. Families may well work at their own rules as a way of managing conflicts, but the effectiveness of these depends on their being worked out and accepted within the family, not imposed from outside.

REMEMBER

As a group, suggest things that "trigger" conflicts and anger in the family and compile a list of them.

(Time guide 10 minutes)

Divide into pairs. Recall situations of conflict between parents and children in which you have been involved *both as parents and as children*. Share your memories of these conflicts, describing how you felt, and, as far as you can, what made you feel like that.

(Time guide 10 minutes)

REFLECT

The group leaders put up a sheet as follows:

Triggers	Feelings as a child	Feelings as a parent

Come together as a group and from your memories begin to fill in the sheet. If you find it hard to find words to describe your feelings, look at the list of words and phrases below.

(Time guide 10 minutes)

FEELINGS THAT MAY UNDERLIE CONFLICTS IN THE FAMILY

Pushed around	Responsible	Frightened
Squashed	Ignored	Anxious
Frustrated	Baffled	Treated like a child
Provoked	Bewildered	Tied down
Mucked about	Amazed	Humiliated
Insulted	Shocked	Aggrieved
Cheated	Embarrassed	Taken for a ride
Let down	Deceived	Taken for granted
Helpless	Exploited	Hopeless
Taken advantage of	Betrayed	

Try to say what made you feel like that. If you think it might help, be ready to ask others in the group what *they* think made you feel like that.

REMEMBER AGAIN

Divide into the same pairs as before, and share with each other your memories of how the conflicts were resolved or aggravated.

(Time guide 10 minutes)

23

REFLECT AGAIN

Come together again as a group. Discuss:

- What were the factors that were helpful in resolving conflicts?
- What were the factors that tended to aggravate them?

(Time guide 10 minutes)

COMPARE

Look at the two Bible passages and questions.

Each member reads the Bible passages silently, and then one member reads them aloud to the whole group. Members then think about the questions silently for a few minutes before beginning to share their answers.

(Time guide 20 minutes)

We have sinned as our ancestors did;
we have been wicked and evil.
Our ancestors in Egypt did not understand God's
wonderful acts;
they forgot the many times he showed them his love,
and they rebelled against the Almighty at the Red Sea . . .
Then they rejected the pleasant land,
because they did not believe God's promise.
They stayed in their tents and grumbled
and would not listen to the LORD . . .
They made themselves impure by their actions
and were unfaithful to God.

So the LORD was angry with his people;
he was disgusted with them.
He abandoned them to the power of the heathen.
and their enemies ruled over them.
They were oppressed by their enemies

and were in complete subjection to them.
Many times the LORD rescued his people,
but they chose to rebel against him
and sank deeper into sin.
Yet the LORD heard them when they cried out,
and he took notice of their distress.
For their sake he remembered his covenant,
and because of his great love he relented.

Psalm 106.6, 7, 24, 25, 39–45

Children, it is your Christian duty to obey your parents, for this is the right thing to do. "Respect your father and mother" is the first commandment that has a promise added: "so that all may go well with you, and you may live a long time in the land."

Parents, do not treat your children in such a way as to make them angry. Instead, bring them up with Christian discipline and instruction.

Ephesians 6.1–4

QUESTIONS FOR DISCUSSION

What does the passage from Psalm 106 tell us about God's conflict with his people, and his feelings towards them?

How do the two passages help us to understand the conflicts and anger in our own families?

RESPOND

Divide into the same pairs as before, and think about the questions below.

Share your answers in pairs. You might like to make a note of them and share them with your partner when you get home.

1. What are the conflicts in your family?

2. Which conflicts may be unavoidable, if things are to be worked out within your family?

3. Which ones can be avoided?

4. In the conflicts which are unavoidable, how do you express your feelings? What effect does this have on your children?

5. In the unnecessary conflicts, how do you get caught up in them? How can they be avoided or diffused?

(Time guide 20 minutes)

Close the meeting with prayer, if appropriate.

BEFORE THE NEXT MEETING

In the next meeting we are going to be thinking about prayer, not only in the sense of speaking to God, but also of other ways of being aware of God. The questions begin by inviting children to talk about experiences that may lead into forms of prayer.

If they are old enough, ask your children:

- What do you find it helpful to do when you are miserable or lonely?
- What do you find it helpful to do when you are feeling angry, or feeling bad because you have done something wrong?
- What do you feel like doing when something really good has happened?

When you have talked with them about this, you might like to ask them about their understanding of prayer. Do they pray? When? What kind of things do they pray about?

If you are asking these questions, it is important that you are willing to answer them yourself, and share your answers with your children.

If your children are younger, are there things you have noticed they do at times of strong feeling? For example, when he is feeling miserable, Tom often goes and sits on the swing in the garden. Are there things you have noticed older children do but which they have not mentioned? As far as you know, do they ever refer to these strong feelings in their spoken prayer?

FIFTH MEETING

SHARING PRAYER WITH OUR CHILDREN

AIM

To help members to recognize and affirm their own experience of prayer, to broaden and develop their prayer life, and to recognize ways of praying into which they can lead their children.

INTRODUCTION

At the start of the meeting you will be asked to say whether you prayed as a child, and if so, how. It will be important for you to restrict yourself to describing what *you actually did* (as far as you can remember) and not get sidetracked into a theoretical discussion about prayer.

Talking about prayer sometimes makes people feel guilty that they do not pray as they should. They realize they no longer pray the way they used to, or were taught to. If it makes you feel guilty, say so, but recognize that this is a basis for growth. You may have outgrown ways of praying that were suitable for you in the past, and may need to learn and work out new ways of praying.

In the second part of the meeting you can look at the different descriptions of prayer on pages 30–32. Some may be familiar, others not. They can help you to see the breadth of meaning of "prayer" in the Christian tradition. You can decide whether these are ways you would like to share with your children.

REMEMBER

As a group, share childhood memories of prayer.

Did you pray as a child? If so, how did you pray?

(Time guide 15 minutes)

REFLECT

Go through the prayer ideas one by one, different people reading them. With each, make sure you understand what is being described. Ask yourself questions like:

• Do I pray in this way?
• Would I find this idea helpful?

When you have read all of them, consider whether there are any other prayer ideas that could be added.

(Time guide 20 minutes)

Reading prayers   Celia has a book of prayers. She likes to sit down in the middle of the morning and read one or two, and think about the pictures alongside them.

Learnt prayers   John has a number of prayers which he knows. He says one of them from time to time. One of his favourites is the prayer of St Francis, "Lord, make me an instrument of thy peace . . ." He often says it in his mind when he is on his way to see someone and he knows it will be a difficult meeting.

Extemporary prayer   Anne goes to a church prayer meeting once a fortnight. A group of them get together for twenty minutes or so and pray by speaking out loud to God. Most days she spends some time praying that way, except that she just thinks the words when she is on her own.

30

Silence Sam likes to have some time when he can be quiet. He likes walking in wild places but also he sometimes sits for a while in his favourite chair and tunes in to what is going on around him. He listens to the sounds, and concentrates on the way his body feels. Then he is able to be still while the world moves around him. He finds it helps him to be whole again.

Special places Some people have places they like to go to occasionally. Jane has a seat in a corner of the park from where she can spend a few minutes looking through to trees at the estate. Mollie likes to go on her own and wander round the ruins of an abbey. There is a headland in Wales from which Jim likes to look at the sea. He tries to get there at least once a year.

Meditation Mark was first taught to meditate by a Franciscan who visited his church on a mission. He sits on a stool, at home, or in church, stills himself and occasionally looks at something that he has deliberately chosen for his meditation. Sometimes it is a candle, or a jug of water, or a flower. His thoughts and his feelings go off in various directions, towards people, Bible stories, sayings of Jesus, and poems, and he gently brings them back to the thing in front of him.

Tongues It was at a big rally that Peter first heard people praying with what seemed to be a language they were making up as they went along. Some time later he received the gift of tongues. Now he often prays that way, finding that it brings him closer to God.

Singing Jackie sings a lot. She sings in a group at her church, and also likes to sing songs around the house, especially when she is on her own.

Imaginative reading Bob likes to read a passage from one of the Gospels, and then imagine what it must have been like being one of the people in the story — what the person would have seen, and heard, and felt like. He finds this often helps him see things in a fresh way.

Awareness Rachel goes to work on the bus. She tries to be aware of the people around her. She notices how they are — happy, worried, fidgety, peaceful, or possibly in pain.

Working Dorothy cleans the church once a month. It takes a couple of hours but she enjoys it, particularly polishing when she is on her own. She loses track of time.

Saying grace Sunday lunch is often the only meal in the week when the whole of the Williams family sits down together. They hold hands and one of them, out loud, thanks God for the meal.

Movement In the service at Ron's church the bread and wine are brought forward from the back of the church during a hymn, together with the collection. Everyone stands and it is always a hymn of praise. This is often a great time for Ron. It is as if he and everyone else in the church is being brought to a great celebration.

Posture When Kevin was a child he was told to kneel down, close his eyes and put his hands together when he prayed. Now he much prefers to sit up in church, with his hands palms up on his knees, and to look at the cross or the window.

COMPARE

Look at the Bible passages describing Jesus' prayer life in Luke's Gospel, perhaps with different people reading each one.

What do these tell us about Jesus' way of praying?

How do they help you to understand about prayer?

(Time guide 20 minutes)

Then Jesus went to Nazareth, where he had been brought up, and on the Sabbath he went as usual to the synagogue.
Luke 4.16

. . . he would go away to lonely places, where he prayed.
Luke 5.16

One day Jesus was praying in a certain place. When he had finished, one of his disciples said to him, "Lord, teach us to pray, just as John taught his disciples."
    Jesus said to them, "When you pray, say this:
    'Father:
    May your holy name be honoured;
    may your Kingdom come.
    Give day by day the food we need.
    Forgive us our sins,
    for we forgive everyone who does us wrong.
    And do not bring us to hard testing.'"   **Luke 11.1–4**

Then [Jesus] took a piece of bread, gave thanks to God, broke it, and gave it to them, saying, "This is my body . . ."
Luke 22.19

Just before his arrest:

Jesus left the city and went, as he usually did, to the Mount of Olives; and the disciples went with him. When he arrived at the place, he said to them, "Pray that you will not fall into temptation."
    Then he went off from them about the distance of a stone's throw and knelt down and prayed. "Father," he said, "if you will, take this cup of suffering away from me. Not my will, however, but your will be done." An angel from heaven appeared to him and strengthened him. In great anguish he prayed even more fervently; his sweat was like drops of blood falling to the ground.
    Rising from his prayer, he went back to the disciples and found them asleep, worn out by their grief. He said to them, "Why are you sleeping? Get up and pray that you will not fall into temptation."
Luke 22.39–46

33

When he was crucified:

Jesus said, "Forgive them, Father! They don't know what they are doing."

Luke 23.34

Jesus cried out in a loud voice, "Father! In your hands I place my spirit!" He said this and died.

Luke 23.46

JESUS AND PRAYER

We don't actually know very much about Jesus' way of praying. The gospels tell us that he would sometimes go off on his own to pray. He would leave everyone else, even his disciples, and go up into the hills, but we do not know how he prayed when he got there.

The gospels make it clear that Jesus prayed in a variety of different ways. He went to the synagogue and joined in the prayers of the local community. The synagogue service would have included both set prayers and prayers which were made up by the leader as he spoke. It would also include the reading of scripture, and a sermon.

At other times Jesus spoke spontaneously to God. In the Garden of Gethsemane he wrestled in his prayer with his conviction of God's love and his awareness that he must die. Also before meals Jesus blessed the bread, like the head of any Jewish household, although he clearly had a particular way of doing it. When the disciples asked Jesus to teach them to pray he gave them a pattern which they could remember easily and say together. Some people find that a good way of praying.

As we think about sharing prayer with our children it is important for us to develop and use the ways of praying that are most helpful to us. Unless we do this we cannot really share prayer with our children. Learning to pray ourselves comes first.

RESPOND

We can share prayer with our children in at least four different contexts. Put these up on a wallsheet.

- An adult with a child: one to one.
- In a family group: small group, mixed ages.
- In a group consisting mainly of children: Sunday School, children's club, school assembly.
- In a church service: large group, mixed ages.

In these different situations different forms of prayer may be appropriate.

Go through the ways of praying that had a positive response from the group and spend a few minutes discussing each.

- Is it a way of praying we could share with our children?
- Is it a way of prayer we would want to share with them?
- If so, how might we do it? In what context would we do it?

In pairs, tell each other of one or two ways of praying that you would like to develop and share with your children. Make any notes you feel you need as reminders.

(Time guide 30 minutes)

The meeting might end with the saying of the Lord's Prayer together.

BEFORE THE FINAL MEETING

There are two aspects to this meeting:

- It is the last meeting of the course, so that the group is ending.
- It looks at the endings our children face, including the final ending — death.

35

To get ready for the first, think about these two questions:

1.   What have you got out of this course?

2.   How do you feel about the group coming to an end?

To get ready for the second, talk with your children about things coming to an end, and how they feel about it. For example, you might ask them: can you think of something you were sad about when it finished? What happened? What was the feeling like? At the end of the conversation you can jot down some notes to help you remember.

With younger children, you can remember and observe how they behave when they are facing an ending, for example, the end of a party, the end of a holiday, leaving playgroup.

FINAL MEETING

ENDINGS

AIM

To bring the meetings of the group to a satisfactory ending, and to help group members to talk to and support their children as they face endings.

INTRODUCTION

Your feelings about the ending of the group meetings are an important part of this final meeting. For some the ending of the course will not be very significant, particularly if they expect to see other members of the group fairly frequently in future. For others, who have valued the group discussions and found them liberating, and do not expect to see much of the other members in future, the ending of the meetings may be quite painful. It is important that they have the chance to express that pain.

Endings in this context include, for example, leaving a school or moving home, and also different kinds of loss, the death of a pet, the loss of a friend.

The session has been planned on two assumptions. The first is that every ending or loss is like "a little death", and the second is that the way we respond to these endings prepares us for the last ending, death.

Adults frequently find it difficult to talk to children about endings, and in particular about death. There are three points it may be helpful for you to remember:

1. There is an immediacy and intensity about the way young children experience and express their feelings. Young children who fall down and cut themselves dissolve into floods of tears. If they are comforted, perhaps by being cuddled by their mother or father, in a few minutes they recover and run off to play again as if nothing had happened. The intensity of the feeling is matched by the speed of recovery. A similar pattern can sometimes be seen in the grief of a child, for example over the death of a pet animal or the loss of a treasured toy. The key factor here is the responsiveness of the adult to the child's feelings at the point of need.

2. For young children death is not a sharp dividing line in the way that it is for adults. For them it is part of the natural pattern of life, and they tend to see life after death as a simple extension of life as they know it. So, for example, a five-year-old, after burying a dead baby rabbit found in the garden, said that it was now playing with Jesus.

3. Remember that our difficulty as adults in talking to children about death reflects our own difficulty in coming to terms with death. Similarly the uncertainty and confusion we adults feel in talking to children about life after death reflects our uncertainty and confusion over our beliefs about life after death and the hope of the resurrection.

REMEMBER

As a group, "brainstorm" as many different kinds of endings or losses as possible. Write them up on a wallsheet.
(Time guide 5 minutes)
In pairs, choose an ending in your life about which you feel deeply, and tell your partner about it.
(Time guide 10 minutes)

38

REFLECT

As a group, focus again on the list of endings and consider which were the most difficult and the least difficult. You might like to put them into categories. Where would you put the ending of this group?

(Time guide 10 minutes)

Thinking of the ending that you shared with your partner a few moments ago, what would you want to remember if you ever had to go through the experience again? Have a few moments of silence, and then reply if you want to. Don't feel you have to discuss any of your answers.

(Time guide 5 minutes)

RESPOND

Consider the three situations below, and the two questions for discussion.

Decide either to discuss one of the situations as a single group; or to divide into sub-groups, each of which can choose the situation it wishes to discuss.

- You are moving home and are leaving a house your child is very fond of, and he or she will be leaving friends he or she is very close to.
- Your pet dog, of which your child is very fond, has been killed in a road accident.
- Your child's grandparent, to whom he or she has become very attached, has died suddenly.

1. How would you break the news to your child(ren)?

2. In what way would you try to support your child(ren) in their loss and grief?

If you divide into sub-groups, each group should share the conclusions it reached.

(Time guide 35 minutes)

An important part of mourning is having the opportunity to affirm what has been valued in the relationship that is ending. So it is suggested that you allow about a quarter of an hour towards the end of the meeting to say what you have valued in the group meetings, and, if you want to, how you feel about them coming to an end. These feelings need to be acknowledged and accepted. It is also important to say if there have been things that have disappointed you in the group meetings, and for this dissatisfaction to be acknowledged and accepted.

If you wish, try to answer these questions in a few sentences.

- What have you valued in the group discussions on Faith in the Family?
- What do you think you have got out of them?
- How are you feeling about their ending?
- Is there anything you feel has been unhelpful or could have been improved?

(Time guide 15 minutes)

BIBLE "ENDINGS"

The Bible passages are used in a slightly different way in this final meeting. In previous meetings the Bible has been used to compare with your own reflections, before you work out how to respond. Here it is used to end the group in a meditative way, to put your feelings about the ending of the group into a wider context. The passages are to be used as an aid to reflection, and no discussion is necessary.

To end the session, five members of the group could read the Bible passages, with a short time of silence for reflection after each reading.

(Time guide 10 minutes)

When Jesus arrived, he found that Lazarus had been buried four days before. Bethany was less than three kilometres from Jerusalem, and many Judaeans had come to see Martha and Mary to comfort them over their brother's death.

When Martha heard that Jesus was coming, she went out to meet him, but Mary stayed in the house. Martha said to Jesus, "If you had been here, Lord, my brother would not have died! But I know that even now God will give you whatever you ask him for."

"Your brother will rise to life," Jesus told her.

"I know," she replied, "that he will rise to life on the last day."

Jesus said to her, "I am the resurrection and the life. Whoever believes in me will live, even though he dies; and whoever lives and believes in me will never die. Do you believe this?"

"Yes, Lord!" she answered. "I do believe that you are the Messiah, the Son of God, who was to come into the world."

After Martha said this, she went back and called her sister Mary privately. "The Teacher is here," she told her, "and is asking for you." When Mary heard this, she got up and hurried out to meet him. (Jesus had not yet arrived in the village, but was still in the place where Martha had met him.) The people who were in the house with Mary, comforting her, followed her when they saw her get up and hurry out. They thought that she was going to the grave to weep there.

Mary arrived where Jesus was, and as soon as she saw him, she fell at his feet. "Lord," she said, "if you had been here, my brother would not have died!"

Jesus saw her weeping, and he saw how the people who were with her were weeping also; his heart was touched, and he was deeply moved.

"Where have you buried him?" he asked them.

"Come and see, Lord," they answered.

Jesus wept. "See how much he loved him!" the people said.

But some of them said, "He gave sight to the blind man, didn't he? Could he not have kept Lazarus from dying?"

John 11.17–37

41

*. . . we want you to know the truth about those who have died,
so that you will not be sad, as are those who have no hope. We
believe that Jesus died and rose again . . .*
I Thessalonians 4.13,14

*For everything there is a season, and a time for every matter
under heaven;*
a time to be born, and a time to die;
a time to plant, and a time to pluck up what is planted;
a time to kill, and a time to heal;
a time to break down, and a time to build up;
a time to weep, and a time to laugh;
a time to mourn, and a time to dance . . .
Ecclesiastes 3.1-4, RSV

Happy are those who know they are spiritually poor;
the Kingdom of heaven belongs to them!
Happy are those who mourn;
God will comfort them!
Matthew 5.3,4

A voice cries out, "Proclaim a message!"
"What message shall I proclaim?" I ask.
"Proclaim that all mankind are like grass;
they last no longer than wild flowers.
Grass withers and flowers fade,
when the LORD sends the wind blowing over them.
People are no more enduring than grass.
Yes, grass withers and flowers fade,
but the word of our God endures for ever." . . .

He strengthens those who are weak and tired.
Even those who are young grow weak;
young men can fall exhausted.
But those who trust in the LORD for help
will find their strength renewed.
They will rise on wings like eagles;
they will run and not get weary;
they will walk and not grow weak.
Isaiah 40.6–8, 29–31

You may like to bring a cake to share with the usual tea or coffee at the end of the meeting. Rituals are important in marking endings.

NOTES FOR GROUP LEADERS

It is worth your while spending some time reading these notes and thinking them through. This will help you lead the group meetings with confidence.

The course is based on the principle of *learning through reflecting on experience* and is designed to enable those taking part:

- to reflect on their experience;
- to use the Bible to help them in understanding their experience;
- where appropriate, to work out what action to take in particular situations.

LEARNING FROM THE COURSE

Through being part of the group, members are likely to gain a good deal of knowledge, both about the subject of the course and about the Christian faith. But imparting this knowledge is not the main aim of the course. It is designed to stimulate the kind of learning which involves personal change.

The course aims to help members to:

- *gain new insights* into themselves and other people;
- *develop new attitudes* towards the situations they face;
- *take new initiatives* in their own lives and in seeking to serve other people in Christ's name.

45

Principles Underlying the Course

Underlying the design of the course are a number of principles, which can be summarized as follows:

People's experience is a rich resource for learning, and reflection on experience is a vital tool in adult learning.

People's feelings have an important role in helping or hindering their learning.

The way people experience the group also has a significant effect on their learning, so that sensitivity to the emotional life of the group is a key element in group leadership.

Biblical and other Christian material can be used to enable people to gain new insights into their everyday experience.

Ideas from the social and human sciences are also valuable in enabling people to understand their everyday experience in new ways.

The Plan of the Course

The course is designed as six meetings of about two hours each, including time for informal conversation at the beginning and end of each session.

It is likely that group members will take some time to get used to the style of the course and the process of learning it is designed to encourage, and to develop the confidence in each other that such learning requires. The first two meetings are designed to help with this.

The Two Themes in the Course

The design of the course is based on the understanding that children's relationships with their parents significantly affect their awareness of God, and their feelings and attitudes towards God.

Based on this understanding, the course has been designed to weave together two themes—the relationships between the parents in the group and their children, and the ways in which the parents try to share their faith in God with the children, for example through prayer and the Bible.

THE FRAMEWORK FOR LEARNING

The meetings of this course are based on a four-stage framework:

Remember
Reflect
Compare
Respond

Remember
The first stage is recalling experience. Sometimes this is done simply by asking members to tell each other about their experience. In some situations activities are suggested to help people to clarify their feelings.

Reflect
The second stage is reflecting on this experience, exploring it in discussion with other members of the group.

What are my reasons for doing this?
What effect is it having on our children?
Why do I feel like this?
What are the issues and principles that this raises?

Compare
In the next stage biblical or other Christian material is often

introduced. It provides a way of putting the experience of God's people through the centuries, and the understanding that has developed as a result of it, alongside our own experience and the way we understand it. As the group begins to grasp the meaning of the passage, this raises new questions about the experience being considered.

- Does the passage suggest new ways of seeing the situation?
- Might we take a different attitude towards it?
- What judgement are we going to make about it now?

Respond
The fourth stage is the conclusion to which the whole session is moving: helping group members respond to what they have learned. This might mean taking some new initiative in sharing their faith with their children. The key questions are:

- Does this make you want to take some action in your own situation?
- If so, what do you think you can usefully do?
- Can the group help you to work out what to do?

The essence is: What am I going to do about this?

Each meeting (except perhaps the first) needs to end with at least some minutes in which the attention of the group is focused on this.

It may be helpful to start each session by asking:

Has anyone tried anything as a result of our discussions that they would like to tell us about?

THE GROUP LEARNING PROCESS

The mood, or "feel" of the group is fundamental to the learning process.

An open, exploratory, questioning mood which encourages members to keep asking themselves and each other such questions as "Why do I/you think/feel/do that?", "What are the consequences of doing that?" will encourage learning. An approach which tries to teach people, or gives neat answers to complex questions, will inhibit learning.

Members will learn at their own pace. They will share difficulties and confidences when they feel ready to do so. If they are hurried or pushed faster than they are ready to go, they will tend to clam up.

If the mood of the group is open and relaxed, and it is ready to accept attitudes without criticizing them, it will encourage members to be open and speak frankly of difficulties and so help them to learn more easily and quickly.

When does the questioning and exploring of someone's statement, which can enable them and the rest of the group to learn, come to be felt as implied criticism which makes the speaker clam up? The judgements leaders make about that are an important part of what they bring to the group.

LEADERSHIP IN LEARNING

In any course which aims at learning involving personal change, the role of those leading the group is crucial.

If the leaders are seeking to gain new insight and are ready to change their own attitudes, they will encourage a climate in which other people expect to learn and change.

If the leaders are not expecting to learn and to change, they act as a damper which suppresses the possible learning and development of members. The leaders' openness to being changed by the group is vital to the group's effectiveness.

The task of the group leaders in this course is:

1. to enable members of the group to learn through gaining new insights into past and present experience;

2. to allow the expression of feelings in a way that is safe for the individual and the group;

3. to encourage reflection on the "meaning" of experience in a flexible and sensitive way, i.e. a way that takes account of individual experience and individual capacity for understanding;

4. to enable members to relate their experience to Christian understanding found in the Bible and other Christian writing.

PRACTICAL QUESTIONS IN LEADING A GROUP

DUAL LEADERSHIP

To lead a group in which the learning is largely derived from the experience of the members is a demanding task. Experience of Faith in the Family groups has shown that there are several advantages in having two people sharing the leadership.

They can plan the meetings together and use their different skills and experience in leading the group. They can take complementary roles in the group meetings, for example, one introducing the activities and ideas while the other focuses on and responds to the feelings expressed by group members. They can bring different perspectives to the group and provide a broader view than either could on her or his own. They can reflect together after each meeting and talk over areas of difficulty. When the group is sticky or discouraging, they can support each other.

In practice these advantages are hard to realize. It takes time to develop a working partnership, and to reflect and plan together, and time is usually at a premium. The two may not "gell" into an easy relationship. Dual leadership may slide into alternate leadership in which the two leaders take alternate sessions without achieving the benefits that are possible when leadership is shared.

However the advantages of shared leadership are great enough to make it worth working to achieve them.

FORMING THE GROUP

People leading groups are generally aware that it is likely to be a demanding task, but may underestimate what is involved in getting the group together. It is wise to start work on forming the group six weeks before the first meeting, to allow plenty of time to invite people and to respond to their questions and hesitations.

ADAPTING THE MATERIAL

How much ground groups cover in a meeting depends on how many there are in the group and how freely they talk. It is up to those leading the group to decide whether to use all the material or to leave some parts out. If you do leave some parts out, reflect on the difference it may have made.

USING FLIPCHARTS AND WALLSHEETS

Writing what is said on a sheet and putting it up where everybody can see it fulfils a number of functions:

- it records the statement or question so that people do not need to remember it;
- writing points down and displaying them gives significance to what is said;

51

- a point can be discussed and questioned in a way that is less threatening to the person who made it;
- it helps people to get an overall view of what has been said and begin to see connections and patterns.

A flipchart can be made easily and cheaply. All you need is:

- a piece of hardboard about 2 ft × 3 ft (40cm × 60cm);
- wall lining paper (used for putting underneath wallpaper, and obtainable from DIY shops);
- 2 large "bulldog" clips;
- a re-usable adhesive such as Bostik "Blu-tack".

Cut the lining paper up to fit the board, flatten the sheets and clip them to the board. The board can be propped up on a low table or armchair, and the sheets flipped over. Large felt-tip pens can be used to write on the sheets.

To display completed sheets, unclip them and use the adhesive to stick them on the wall. They can be removed carefully at the end of the meeting without damaging what they have been stuck to.

USING THE HOME ACTIVITIES

The group preparation material contains suggestions for things members can do with their children during the week, to prepare for the next meeting. This can add a great deal to the value of the course. Not only may they understand their children better, but it should encourage and foster a pattern of sharing thoughts between adults and children for the future.

It is therefore worth spending a few minutes at the end of each meeting drawing members' attention to what is suggested and checking that they understand it. If some are hesitant or confused, they need to be given the chance to express this. A few moments' discussion may overcome it, and enable them to go ahead. If they do not express their hesitancy or confusion, they may just let things slide and do nothing.

If possible the leaders themselves should share these activities with their own children between sessions. Example is influential.

REFLECTING ON THE GROUP MEETINGS

Reflecting on the group meetings afterwards is an essential part of leading the group. Learning from the experience of what has happened, you will be able to adapt your leadership in response to the developing life of the group.

After each meeting jot down your answers to as many of these questions as you can. Rough notes made quickly, before your impressions are buried by everything else that happens to you, can be invaluable. Further reflections can be added later.

Which meeting was it?
Who was there? (Or who was missing?)
What was your aim in leading the group?
Which part did people find most interesting?
What were the main issues for group members?
What was the mood of the group? Did it help or hinder people to learn?
What were the most important things group members learned?
What were the most important things you learned?
What links did people make between their experience and Christian ideas?

PREPARING YOURSELF TO LEAD THE GROUP

This meeting is designed to be used by the two leaders of the group.

Share with each other your experience of childhood.

- Was yours a happy childhood?
- What made it happy? What made it unhappy?
- How has it influenced you as an adult?

Take about five minutes each telling the other.

Recall a religious experience you had as a child and describe it to each other. As far as you can recall, say:

how old you were; where you were; what happened; what you felt; why you think it made such an impression on you.

Allow about five minutes each to describe it to each other.

Discuss together:

- Has this reminded you of what it is like being a child?
- If so, what has it reminded you of?

Spend ten minutes discussing this.

Tell each other briefly about your own children. Allow about five minutes each for this.

Each of you focuses on one incident or situation that is fairly recent, in which you have come into conflict with one of your own children. Tell each other what happened.

- What was the conflict about?
- How did you feel at the time?
- How did you feel afterwards?
- As far as you can tell, why did your child behave as he or she did?
- What did he or she feel at the time?
- What did he or she feel afterwards?

Allow about ten minutes each to tell the other.

Reflect together on the whole meeting.

- How did you feel doing these activities?

- Were you conscious of any difficulties?
- How would you feel leading a group in which people found it difficult to share their experience in this way? Or expressed strong disagreement with you, or each other?
- How would you react?

If you wish, end the meeting by praying together.

FURTHER READING

BENCE K   **Turn Off the TV**   Marshall Pickering

BRIDGER F   **Children Finding Faith**   Scripture Union

CARDWELL R   **Helping Children to Pray**   Grail
Publications

COPLEY T   **Onward Christian Parents**   Church House
Publishing

FREEMAN M   **We Always Put a Candle in the Window**
National Society/Church House Publishing

GRIGGS D & P   **Using the Bible with All Ages Together**
Bible Society

HALL D B   **Using the Bible with Children**   Bible Society

HUGHES J   **Questions Children Ask**   Lion Publishing

HUGHES J   **Will My Rabbit Go to Heaven? And Other
Questions Children Ask**   Lion Publishing

KING J   **Making Time for the Family (and Other
Questions)**   Scripture Union

MASPERO S   **Families are for Growing**   Mothers' Union

MELLOR H   **How to Encourage Family Worship**
Scripture Union

PORTER D   **Children at Risk**   Kingsway

TURK M (editor)   **Children in the Way**   Church House
Publishing
Leaves on the Tree   National Society/Church House
Publishing

RESOURCES FOR BIBLE USE
WITH CHILDREN

Bibles for children
The Good News Children's Bible (Bible Society)
Children's Picture Bible (New International Version, Hodder)
A First Bible (Simon & Schuster, *2 volumes*)

For young children
Open House Books (Bible Society) – *board books retelling
    well known Bible stories*
Favourite Bible Stories (Bible Society)
Little Fish Books (Scripture Union)
Palm Tree Bible Stories (Palm Tree Press)
Rainbow Books (Church House Publishing)
Bible Storyboards (Bible Society) — *play-tray jigsaws, each
    telling a Bible story*
Ladybird Bible Books
Teddy Horsley Books (Bible Society)
"Talkabout" Books (Bible Society)
King's Donkey Series (Palm Tree Press)

For children aged 8–13
Adventure Story Bible (Bible Society) — *a series of Bible
    story books*
The Lion Book of Bible Stories and Prayers (Lion Publishing)
Praise: Songs and Prayers from the Bible Retold for Children
    (Collins)
Listen! Themes from the Bible Retold for Children (Collins)
    — *also available as four booklets*
The Bible Story (Brian Wildsmith, Oxford)
Do it Yourself Cartoons (Bible Society)
The Lion Children's Bible

For teenagers and adults
Winding Quest: the Heart of the Old Testament in Plain
    English (A T Dale, Oxford)
New World (A T Dale, Oxford)
City of Gold and Other Stories from the Old Testament
    (Peter Dickinson, Gollancz)
New Life Bible (GNB and NIV versions, Bible Society)

Video
Messages from the Memorybanks (Bible Society)
Children's Video Bible (Oxford Vision)
Bible Storygraphics (Bible Society)

Bible Study notes and materials
Bible Society, the Bible Reading Fellowship and Scripture
Union are all useful sources. BRF's starter series *A Way In*,
by J Davies, is recommended.

General
Public libraries usually have a selection of background books
for varying requirements. Two clear and well illustrated
background books are the Lion Handbook of the Bible and
the Lion Encyclopaedia of the Bible.